The Great Divide

MEN AND WOMEN
AT THE EDGE OF
THE GENDER GAP

ARIEL BOOKS

ANDREWS AND MCMEEL
KANSAS CITY

The Great Divide

MEN AND WOMEN

AT THE EDGE OF

THE GENDER GAP

Contents

Introduction

**Sometimes I wonder if men and women really suit each other.
Perhaps they should live next door and
just visit now and then.**

KATHARINE HEPBURN

The great divide . . . men vs. women—will it ever end? Will he ever do his share of the housework? Will she ever learn proper auto maintenance? For some couples, this isn't a case of "he says tomato, I say tomahto," it's downright war!

Throughout history, many men and women have successfully leaped the gender gap. Recently, for instance, men have become more active in parenting, and women have forged new careers in the workplace. But in day-to-day living, some will swear that the gender gap is still there—and just as wide as ever. Men debate, "Should I open the car door for my date?" Women wonder, "Should I offer to pay for lunch?" Minor dilemmas like these are often just forerunners of the major issues that divide the sexes. And they illustrate just how slippery our footing is at the edge of the gender gap.

Will we ever bridge the gap entirely? Do we want to? Are men and women really that different? This lively volume addresses those questions and many more. Expect to be enraged, enlightened, and amused by the comments of the men and women included here, but don't expect a verdict: the jury is still out on the gender gap case.

....

Part One: The Gap

Man is a creature who lives not upon bread alone, but principally by catchwords; and the little rift between the sexes is astonishingly widened by simply teaching one set of catchwords to the girls and another to the boys.

ROBERT LOUIS STEVENSON

The perfect hostess will see to it that the works of male and female authors be properly separated on her bookshelves. Their proximity, unless they happen to be married, should not be tolerated.

LADY GOUGH

The two most common causes of divorce?
Men and women.

EDDIE CANTOR

What are little boys made of?
Frogs and snails
And puppy-dogs' tails,
That's what little boys are made of.
What are little girls made of?
Sugar and spice
And all that's nice,
That's what little girls are made of.

J. O. HALLIWELL

After an acquaintance of ten minutes many women will exchange confidences that a man would not reveal to a lifelong friend.

PAGE SMITH

The law of heredity is that all undesirable traits come from the other parent.

ANONYMOUS

Women have just as much right to an uninterrupted career as men, and fathers have just as much responsibility as mothers for caring for their children or deciding who will care for them.

DR. BENJAMIN SPOCK

A successful man is one who makes more money than his wife can spend. A successful woman is one who can find such a man.

LANA TURNER

Men, too, both fear and
long for what will happen
when women can really
say what they want.

DOROTHY DINNERSTEIN

When a man gets up to speak,
people listen then look. When a
woman gets up, people *look*;
then, if they like what they see,
they listen.

PAULINE FREDERICK

I tell you, the great divide is still with us, the awful split, the Us and Them. Like a rubber band tautened to the snapping point, the polarization of the sexes continues, because we lack the courage to face our likenesses and admit to our real need.

COLETTE DOWLING

Instead of this absurd division into sexes they ought to class people as static and dynamic.

EVELYN WAUGH

It is said, for instance, that men are innately more aggressive than women. But conditioning, not sex hormones, makes them that way. Anyone seeing women at a bargain-basement sale—where aggression is viewed as appropriate, even endearing—sees aggression that would make Attila the Hun turn pale.

ESTELLE R. RAMEY

A man is as old as he's feeling,
A woman as old as she looks.

MORTIMER COLLINS

♂ ♀

Men seem to kick friendship around like a football, but it doesn't seem to crack. Women treat it as glass and it goes to pieces.

ANNE MORROW LINDBERGH

♀ ♂

That man knew what it was all about, it seems to me, who said that a good marriage was one made between a blind wife and a deaf husband.

MONTAIGNE

Man for the field and woman for the hearth:
Man for the sword and for the needle she:
Man with the head and woman with the heart:
Man to command and woman to obey;
All else confusion.

ALFRED, LORD TENNYSON

Women fall in love through their ears and men through their eyes.

WOODROW WYATT

If you want anything said, ask a man. If you want anything done, ask a woman.

MARGARET THATCHER

By the time you say you're his,
Shivering and sighing
And he vows his passion is
Infinite, undying—
Lady, make a note of this:
One of you is lying.

DOROTHY PARKER

The first thing that strikes the careless observer is that women are unlike men. They are "the opposite sex"— (though why "opposite" I do not know; what is the "neighboring sex"?).

DOROTHY L. SAYERS

Love is the history of a woman's life; it is an episode in man's.

MADAME DE STAËL

Women speak because they wish to speak, whereas a man speaks only when driven to speech by something outside himself—like, for instance, he can't find any clean socks.

JEAN KERR

A married couple are well suited when both partners usually feel the need for a quarrel at the same time.

JEAN ROSTAND

Today the hemisphere of the public has been assigned to the male and the hemisphere of the private to the female. Each sex has become a symbol for its territory. The conflict between them can then be seen as a reflection of the longing of each to be part of the other's sphere, to link the public with the private in our schizoid world, to embrace the whole of life.

NANCY REEVES

I don't think men and women were meant to live together. They are totally different animals.

DIANA DORS

$\male$ $\female$

A man is designed to walk three miles in the rain to phone for help when the car breaks down—and a woman is designed to say, "You took your time" when he comes back dripping wet.

VICTORIA WOOD

$\female$

Now one of the great reasons why so many husbands and wives make shipwreck of their lives together is because a man is always seeking for happiness, while a woman is on a perpetual still hunt for trouble.

DOROTHY DIX

Man and woman are two locked caskets, of which each contains the key to the other.

ISAK DINESEN

Sure men were born to lie, and women to believe them.

JOHN GAY

It is apparent that we cannot speak of inferiority and superiority but only of specific differences in aptitudes and personality between the sexes. These differences are largely the result of cultural and other experiential factors.

ANNE ANASTASI

To be happy with a man you must understand him a lot and love him a little. To be happy with a woman you must love her a lot and not try to understand her at all.

HELEN ROWLAND

There is perhaps one human being in a thousand who is passionately interested in the job for the job's sake. The difference is that if that one person in a thousand is a man, we say, simply, that he is passionately keen on his job; if she is a woman, we say she is a freak.

DOROTHY L. SAYERS

Men and women, women
and men. It will never
work.

ERICA JONG

Women represent the triumph of matter over mind, just as men represent the triumph of mind over morals.

OSCAR WILDE

Men readily interrupt the speech of women, and women allow the interruption.

SUSAN BROWNMILLER

Whpen men and women agree, it is only in their conclusions; their reasons are always different.

GEORGE SANTAYANA

Women tend to qualify more than men. They put "perhaps" and "I think" and use diminutives more than men.

GAIL GODWIN

Men are generally more law-abiding than women. Women have the feeling that since they didn't make the rules, the rules have nothing to do with them.

DIANE JOHNSON

When a man confronts catastrophe on the road, he looks in his purse—but a woman looks in her mirror.

MARGARET TURNBULL

To the mere superficial observer, it would seem that man was sent into this breathing world for the purpose of enjoyment—woman for that of trial and of suffering.

SARAH WENTWORTH MORTON

This is courtship all the world over—the man all tongue; the woman all ears.

EMILY GOWAN MURPHY

Did little girls have to be as good as that?" Laura asked, and Ma said: "It was harder for little girls. Because they had to behave like little ladies all the time, not only on Sundays. Little girls could never slide downhill, like boys. Little girls had to sit in the house and stitch on samplers."

LAURA INGALLS WILDER

If it's a woman, it's caustic; if it's a man, it's authoritative. If it's a woman, it's too often pushy; if it's a man it's aggressive in the best sense of the word.

BARBARA WALTERS

When Eve ate this particular apple, she became aware of her own womanhood, mentally. And mentally she began to experiment with it. She has been experimenting ever since. So has man. To the rage and horror of both of them.

D. H. LAWRENCE

Men are taught to
apologize for their
weaknesses, women for
their strengths.

LOIS WYSE

Man/Woman automatically means great/small, superior/inferior . . . the whole conglomeration of symbolic systems—everything, that is, that's spoken, everything that's organized as discourse, art, religion, the family, language, everything that seizes us, everything that acts on us—it is all ordered around hierarchical oppositions that come back to the man/woman opposition.

HÉLÈNE CIXOUS

Men, the very best of
men, can only suffer,
while women can endure.

DINAH MARIA MULOCK CRAIK

Anyone who believes that men and women have the same mindset hasn't lived on earth. A man thinks that everything he does is wonderful; a woman has *doubts*.

MARGO KAUFMAN

A woman may not hit a ball stronger than a man, but it is different. I prize that difference.

LOUISE NEVELSON

A lady tried to embroil Sir John Mahaffy in a feminist argument by saying to him, "You are a man. I am a woman. What is the essential difference between us?"

"Madam," he replied, "I can't conceive."

SIR JOHN PENTLAND MAHAFFY

The only difference between men and women is that women are able to create new little human beings in their bodies while simultaneously writing books, driving tractors, working in offices, planting crops—in general, do everything men do.

ERICA JONG

I didn't want to be a boy, ever, but I was outraged that his height and intelligence were graces for him and gaucheries for me.

JANE RULE

Men are as afraid of us as we are of them, although few men are willing to say so. (Disclosing state secrets is treason.)

VICTORIA BILLINGS

I have never in all my various travels seen but two sorts of people, and those very like one another; I mean men and women, who always have been and ever will be the same.

LADY MARY WORTLEY MONTAGUE

Women may think like men, act like men, live the rules of the male world, and think they live in the male world until something happens that shows how wide the chasm really is.

JESSIE SHIRLEY BERNARD

There is more difference
within the sexes than
between them.

IVY COMPTON-BURNETT

**Yang—positive cosmic force,
the heavens, man.
Yin—negative cosmic force,
earth, woman.**

CONFUCIUS

W here young boys plan for what they will achieve and attain, young girls plan for whom they will achieve and attain.

CHARLOTTE PERKINS GILMAN

♂   ♀

What is most beautiful in virile men is something feminine; what is most beautiful in feminine women is something masculine.

SUSAN SONTAG

♀   ♂

I think what I would ideally like to see in our society is that sex become an ascribed rather than an achieved status. That one is simply born a girl or a boy and that's it. And no worry about an activity's defeminizing or emasculating one.

DAVID REISMAN

It is a woman's business
to get married as soon as
possible, and a man's to
keep unmarried as
long as he can.

GEORGE BERNARD SHAW

The reason that husbands and wives do not understand each other is because they belong to different sexes.

DOROTHY DIX

I object to anything that divides the two sexes. My main point is this: human development has now reached a point at which sexual difference has become a thing of altogether minor importance. We make too much of it; we are men and women in the second place, human beings in the first.

OLIVE SCHREINER

Man has his will—but
woman has her way!

OLIVER WENDELL HOLMES

When women try to initiate a free-wheeling discussion by asking, "What do you think?" men often think they are being asked to decide.

DEBORAH TANNEN

It is so many years now since Adam and Eve were first together in the garden, that it seems a great pity that we have not learned better how to please one another . . . I wish that once, in all the time of men and women, two ambassadors could meet in a friendly mind and come to understand each other.

ISAK DINESEN

Nobody will ever win the battle of the sexes. There's just too much fraternizing with the enemy.

HENRY (ALFRED) KISSINGER

Between man and woman there is little difference, but *vive la différence*.

FRENCH PROVERB

Part Two: On Men

The best way to get most husbands to do something is to suggest that perhaps they're too old to do it.

SHIRLEY MACLAINE

♂ ♀

**Energy is more attractive
than beauty in a man.**

LOUISA MAY ALCOTT

♀ ♂

I've been married to one Marxist and one Fascist, and neither one would take the garbage out.

LEE GRANT

Gee, I get tired of hearing that boys can do a certain thing but girls can't.

KATE TOMIBE

A diplomat is a man who always remembers a woman's birthday but never remembers her age.

ROBERT FROST

Trust your husband, adore your husband, and get as much as you can in your own name.

JOAN RIVERS

Blessed is the man who, having nothing to say, abstains from giving in words evidence of the fact.

GEORGE ELIOT

I wouldn't trust my husband with a young woman for five minutes, and he's been dead for twenty-five years.

BRENDAN BEHAN'S MOTHER

Boys pride themselves on their drab clothing, their droopy socks, their smeared and inky skin: dirt, for them, is almost as good as wounds. They work at acting like boys. They call each other by their last names, draw attention to any extra departures from cleanliness . . . There always seem to be more of them in the room than there actually are.

MARGARET ATWOOD

The only time a woman
really succeeds in
changing a man is when
he is a baby.

NATALIE WOOD

QUESTION: How many men does it take to change a light bulb?

ANSWER: Five. One to force it with a hammer and four to go out for more bulbs.

ANONYMOUS

If you never want to see a man again, say, "I love you, I want to marry you. I want to have your children . . ."—they leave skid marks.

RITA RUDNER

Men prefer these living
dolls to real women out
of fear.

ELIZA LYNN LINTON

Man forgives woman anything save the wit to outwit him.

MINNA ANTRIM

Men build bridges and throw railroads across deserts, and yet they contend successfully that the job of sewing on a button is beyond them. Accordingly, they don't have to sew buttons.

HEYWOOD BROUN

There are no father-in-law
jokes.

BERNICE SANDLER

If there is anything
disagreeable going on,
men are sure to get
out of it.

JANE AUSTEN

Northanger Abbey

My ancestors wandered lost in the wilderness for forty years because even in biblical times, men would not stop to ask for directions.

ELAYNE BOOSLER

Beware of the man who praises women's liberation; he is about to quit his job.

ERICA JONG

Men have no experience "taking hints." Your attempts at subtlety—which work so well with your female friends—will get you nowhere with your husbands.

ROSEANNE ARNOLD

There are only two kinds
of men—the dead and
the deadly.

HELEN ROWLAND

The man who gets on best with women is the one who knows best how to get on without them.

CHARLES BAUDELAIRE

In passing, also, I would like to say that the first time Adam had a chance he laid the blame on women.

LADY NANCY ASTOR

A man has by nature the urge to understand the things he has to deal with; small boys show a predilection for pulling their toys to pieces to find out what they look like inside or how they work.

EMMA JUNG

A man expects his wife to be perfect—and to understand why he isn't.

ANONYMOUS

Woman's work! Housework's the hardest work in the world. That's why men won't do it.

EDNA FERBER

Men are creatures with
two legs and eight hands.

JAYNE MANSFIELD

Women] are the real sportsmen. They don't have to be constantly building up frail egos by large public performances like over-tipping the hat-check girl, speaking fluent French to the Hungarian waiter, and sending back the wine to be recooled.

PHYLLIS MCGINLEY

It's all right for a perfect stranger to kiss your hand as long as he's perfect.

MAE WEST

If love means never having to say you're sorry, then marriage means always having to say everything twice. Husbands, due to an unknown quirk of the universe, never hear you the first time.

ESTELLE GETTY

A man is *so* in the way in the house.

ELIZABETH CLEGHORN GASKELL

On American men: "They have wonderful minds. So much is stored inside—all those sports scores and so on."

JANE SEYMOUR

Men don't know much about women. We do know when they're happy, we know when they're crying, and we know when they're pissed off. We just don't know in what order these are gonna come at us.

EVAN DAVIS

Men don't tell enough details.

DEBORAH TANNEN

The trouble about man is twofold. He cannot learn truths which are too complicated; he forgets truths which are too simple.

DAME REBECCA WEST

Two things a man cannot hide: that he is drunk, and that he is in love.

ANTIPHANES

Oddly enough, while men cannot remember basic facts—like your dress size or your anniversary—they can recite from memory every statistic from every football game that took place during the last six years.

ROSEANNE ARNOLD

I refuse to consign the whole male sex to the nursery. I insist on believing that some men are my equals.

BRIGID BROPHY

Men will *not* change, *unless they have to.*

DORA RUSSELL

It is always incomprehensible to a man that a woman should ever refuse an offer of marriage.

JANE AUSTEN

Men don't know anything about pain; they've never experienced labor, cramps, or a bikini wax.

NAN TISDALE

Nice guys can't get cabs.

MERLE SHAIN

I was exploring the ways women and men related to me as Dorothy and I'd never been related to that way before in my life—having men meet me, say hello and immediately start looking over my shoulder trying to find an attractive woman! . . . I would get very hostile: I wanted to get even with them.

DUSTIN HOFFMAN

He is every other inch a
gentleman.

DAME REBECCA WEST

QUESTION: What is a man's idea of a seven-course meal?

ANSWER: A hot dog and a six-pack.

ANONYMOUS

Men are unable to admit that they are wrong, no matter how lightweight the issue.

SONYA FRIEDMAN

If men can run the world, why can't they stop wearing neckties? How intelligent is it to start the day by tying a little noose around your neck?

LINDA ELLERBEE

Women's liberation is just a lot of foolishness. It's the men who are discriminated against. They can't bear children. And no one's likely to do anything about that.

GOLDA MEIR

Men will talk, sometimes in complete sentences but more often not, to women on the street. In my case, I hear a lot of "Yo, Red!" Exactly what am I supposed to do with a comment like Yo, Red? Yell back "Yo, Bald!" or "Yo, Short!"

DORIAN YEAGER

Life isn't fair to us men. When we are born, our mothers get the compliments and the flowers. When we are married, our brides get the presents and the publicity. When we die, our widows get the life insurance and winters in Florida. What do women want to be liberated from?

ANONYMOUS

Men often wonder what it is they have done wrong.

ANNA FORD

I think the men's movement is a great idea. I just wish part of the movement they made was to clean the bathtub.

ANONYMOUS

It isn't tying himself to one woman that a man dreads when he thinks of marrying; it's separating himself from all the others.

HELEN ROWLAND

The majority of husbands remind me of an orangutan trying to play the violin.

HONORÉ DE BALZAC

Nobody works as hard for his money as the man who marries it.

KIN HUBBARD

There's nothing so stubborn as a man when you want him to do something.

JEAN GIRADOUX

The Madwoman of Chaillot

The (men) like to be heroes.

FAY WELDON

Latins are tenderly enthusiastic. In Brazil they throw flowers at you. In Argentina they throw themselves.

MARLENE DIETRICH

Men have always been
afraid that women could
get along without them.

MARGARET MEAD

The man who can't understand why women can't be more like men is the same man who will complain if women change their behavior.

VICTORIA BILLINGS

Have you not heard
When a man marries, dies, or
turns Hindoo,
His best friends hear no more
of him?

PERCY BYSSHE SHELLEY

One-third mush and two-thirds Eleanor.

ALICE ROOSEVELT

LONGWORTH

(on Franklin D. Roosevelt)

The bravest thing that men do is love women.

MORT SAHL

Men frequently annoy women by usurping or switching the topic.

DEBORAH TANNEN

Women are never
disarmed by compliments.
Men always are.

OSCAR WILDE

QUESTION: What's a man's idea of helping you with the housework?

ANSWER: Lifting his legs so you can vacuum.

ANONYMOUS

Men are more conventional than women
and much slower to change their ideas.

KATHLEEN NORRIS

Are men afraid we will mock them?

RITA MAE BROWN

QUESTION: Why is it good that there are female astronauts?

ANSWER: Because when the crew gets lost in space, at least a woman will ask for directions.

ANONYMOUS

Positive Reinforcement is hugging your husband when he does a load of laundry. Negative Reinforcement is telling him he used too much detergent.

DR. JOYCE BROTHERS

Very few men care to have
the obvious pointed out
to them by a woman.

MARGARET BAILLIE

SAUNDERS

The husband who wants a happy marriage should learn to keep his mouth shut and his checkbook open.

GROUCHO MARX

♂

Whenever you want to marry someone, go have lunch with his ex-wife.

SHELLEY WINTERS

Marrying a man is like buying something you've been admiring for a long time in a shop window. You may love it when you get it home, but it doesn't always go with everything else in the house.

JEAN KERR

Unless your mate goes by the name of "John-Boy," chances are he spent his entire childhood mastering the fine art of chore avoidance. This is the essential male pastime, on which all of those lesser avocations—fishing, Monday Night Football, global imperialism—are founded.

AARON GELL

A man admires the woman who makes him think, but he keeps away from her. He likes the woman who makes him laugh. He loves the girl who hurts him. But he marries the woman who flatters him.

NELLIE B. STULL

What's with you men? Would hair stop growing on your chest if you asked directions somewhere?

ERMA BOMBECK

Men are subconsciously
afraid of women!

NELLIE MCCLUNG

The success of any man
with any woman is apt to
displease even his best
friends.

MADAME DE STAËL

Getting along with men isn't what's truly important. The vital knowledge is how to get along with a man, one man.

PHYLLIS MCGINLEY

Men are frightened by women's humor, because they think when women are alone, they're making fun of men.

NICOLE HOLLANDER

I have yet to hear a man ask for advice on how to combine marriage and a career.

GLORIA STEINEM

When men talk about defense, they always claim to be protecting women and children, but they never ask the women and children what they think.

PAT SCHROEDER

I am assuming that what men watch and read and write is nobler than what women watch. Baseball is not nobler.

JANE O'REILLY

If a man is vain, flatter. If timid, flatter. If boastful, flatter. In all history, too much flattery never lost a gentleman.

KATHRYN CRAVENS

Y**ou're** fooling yourself if you think you've got new and improved males because you see three or four dudes out there doing diapers and dishes.

BILL COSBY

Many men have little use for small talk.

DEBORAH TANNEN

I only like two kinds of men:
domestic and imported.

MAE WEST

If they could put one man on the moon, why can't they put them all?

ANONYMOUS

To women, we are like big dogs that talk.

LARRY MILLER

There will be some men who under no circumstances can allow a woman to pay a check. By all means, allow him to pay for his own outdated view of chivalry.

DEE WEDEMEYER

What fractures me about most men is that they can't live without male approval.

RITA MAE BROWN

It is ridiculous to think you can spend your entire life with one person. Three is about the right number. Yes, I imagine three husbands would do it.

CLARE BOOTHE LUCE

Part Three: Ouch! Who Said That?

He must have had a magnificent build before his stomach went in for a career of its own.

MARGARET HALSEY

Nature intended women to be our slaves. . .
They are our property, we are not theirs. . . .
They belong to us, just as a tree which bears fruit
belongs to the gardener. What a mad idea to
demand equality for women! . . . Women are
nothing but machines for producing children.

NAPOLÉON BONAPARTE

QUESTION: What's the fastest way to lose 180 ugly pounds?

ANSWER: Throw the bum out.

ANONYMOUS

♂

The wife ought not to have any feelings of her own but join with her husband in his moods whether serious, playful, thoughtful, or joking.

PLUTARCH

♀

HUSBAND: What can I do to make sex better for you?

WIFE: Leave town.

ANONYMOUS

Women are stronger than men
—they do not die of wisdom.
They are better than men
because they do not seek wisdom.
They are wiser than men because
they know less and understand more.

JAMES STEPHENS

Women want mediocre
men, and men are
working hard to be as
mediocre as possible.

MARGARET MEAD

Υou are not permitted to kill a woman who has injured you, but nothing forbids you to reflect that she is growing older every minute.

A M B R O S E   B I E R C E

Most men want their wives to have a jobette.

GLORIA STEINEM

♂

QUESTION: Why is psychoanalysis so much quicker for men than for women?

ANSWER: Because when it's time to go back to childhood, he's already there.

ANONYMOUS

♀

Women are not much, but they are the best other sex we have.

DON HEROLD

♂

As long as you know that
most men are like children
you know everything.

COCO CHANEL

♀

All a woman has to do in this world is contained within the duties of a daughter, a sister, a wife, and a mother.

SIR RICHARD STEELE

I discovered that even now men prefer women to be less informed, less able, less talkative, and certainly less self-centered than they are themselves; so I generally obliged them.

JAN MORRIS

Men are weak and constantly need reassurance, so now that they fail to find adulation in the opposite sex, they're turning to each other. Less and less do men need women. More and more do gentlemen prefer gentlemen.

ANITA LOOS

♂

**The generality of women
appear to me as children whom
I would rather give a sugar
plum than my time.**

JOHN KEATS

♀

You can talk to a man
about any subject. He
won't understand, but
you can talk to him.

ANONYMOUS

A woman's mind is cleaner than a man's; she changes it more often.

OLIVER HERFORD

A loving wife will do anything for her husband except stop criticizing and trying to improve him.

J. B. PRIESTLEY

Girls should always be submissive, but mothers should not always be inexorable. . . . Indeed I should not be sorry if sometimes she were allowed to exercise a little cunning, not to elude punishment but to escape having to obey. Guile is a natural gift of her sex; and being convinced that all natural dispositions are good and right in themselves, I think that this one should be cultivated like the rest. The characteristic cunning with which women are endowed is an equitable compensation for their lesser strength.

JEAN JACQUES ROUSSEAU

I never married because I have three pets at home that answer the same purpose as a husband. I have a dog that growls every morning, a parrot that swears all afternoon, and a cat that comes home late at night.

MARIE CORELLI

Her only flair is in her nostrils.

PAULINE KAEL

Never feel remorse for what you have thought about your wife; she has thought much worse things about you.

JEAN ROSTAND

Nothing is more intolerable than a wealthy woman.

JUVENAL

When you see what some girls marry, you realize how they must hate to work for a living.

HELEN ROWLAND

♂

If American men are obsessed with money, American women are obsessed with weight. The men talk of gain, the women talk of loss, and I do not know which talk is the more boring.

MARYA MANNES

♀

There are only two things
I dislike about her—
her face.

ANONYMOUS

I love Mickey Mouse more than any woman I've ever known.

WALT DISNEY

But what is woman? Only one of nature's agreeable blunders.

A B R A H A M   C O W L E Y

God made man, and then said I can do better than that and made woman.

ADELA ROGERS ST. JOHN

Cherish your husband's person and make sure you keep him in clean linen, this being your office. For men have to look after things outside the house and husbands have to go abroad in all sorts of weather, at times getting soaked in rain, at times dry, and sometimes bathed in sweat.

ANONYMOUS

Because men are simple, they are not physically capable of handling more than one task at a time. Women can easily cook dinner, feed the baby, and talk on the phone all at once. Were a man to try this, he would probably explode.

ROSEANNE ARNOLD

Man, but not woman, is made in the image of God. It is plain from this that women should be subject to their husbands, and should be as slaves.

GRATIAN

Why was man created on the last day?
So that he can be told, when pride possesses
him: God created the gnat before thee.

THE TALMUD

Men really have strange
emotions and behave in
the most bizarre ways.

SEI SHONAGON

Frailty, thy name is woman!

WILLIAM SHAKESPEARE

You don't know a woman until you've met her in court.

NORMAN MAILER

Women's virtue is man's greatest invention.

CORNELIA OTIS SKINNER

Men have broad and large chests, and small narrow hips, and more understanding than women, who have but small and narrow breasts, and broad hips, to the end they should remain at home, sit still, keep house, and bear and bring up children.

MARTIN LUTHER

I have learned valuable information. I have learned that the discussion of the cultural value of history and kindred topics will not get one very far, no matter how clever and apparently serious-minded the gentleman may be. I have learned that one must talk vivaciously, and on such subjects as football. One must laugh and talk about trivial and foolish things.

MARION TAYLOR

I'm not a believer in equality and my attitude is that women are supposed to be pretty and nice. A woman should be a woman.

JIM DAVIDSON

♂

Mistresses we keep for pleasure, concubines for daily attendance upon our persons, wives to bear us legitimate children and to be our faithful housekeepers.

DEMOSTHENES

♀

The evidence indicates that woman is, on the whole, biologically superior to man.

ASHLEY MONTAGU

One tongue is sufficient for a woman.

JOHN MILTON

If a woman has her Ph.D. in physics, has mastered in quantum theory, plays flawless Chopin, was once a cheerleader, and is now married to a man who plays baseball, she will forever be "former cheerleader married to star athlete."

MARYANNE ELLISON SIMMONS

♂

Nothing is so silly as the expression of a man who is being complimented.

ANDRÉ GIDE

♀

Henry VII . . . He didn't get divorced, he just had their heads chopped off when he got tired of them. That's a good way to get rid of a woman—no alimony.

TED TURNER

First time you buy a house you see how pretty the paint is and buy it. The second time you look to see if the basement has termites. It's the same with men.

LUPE VELEZ

The male is a domestic
animal which, if treated
with firmness and kind-
ness, can be trained to
do most things.

JILLY COOPER

I tended to place my wife
under a pedestal.

WOODY ALLEN

If a woman gets nervous, she'll eat or go shopping. A man will attack a country—it's a whole other way of thinking.

ELAYNE BOOSLER

♂

I think that the women who can get beyond the feeling of having to correct history will save a lot of time. The women who are trying to correct man's nature are wasting their time . . . in men's heads everything's still the same . . . I don't care about men. I've given up on them, personally.

MARGUERITE DURAS

♀

224

Do not put such unlimited power into the hands of husbands. Remember, all men would be tyrants if they could.

ABIGAIL ADAMS

♂

One does *not* hug boys.

HENRIETTE DESSAULLES

♀

Before marriage, a man declares that he would lay down his life to serve you; after marriage, he won't even lay down his newspaper to talk to you.

HELEN ROWLAND

Wealth makes them lavish, wit knavish, beauty effeminate, poverty deceitful, and deformity ugly. Therefore, of me take this counsel: Esteem of men as of a broken reed, mistrust them still, and then you well shall speed.

JANE ANGER

Literature cannot be the business of a woman's life, and it ought not to be. The more she is engaged in her proper duties, the less leisure she will have for it, even as an accomplishment and recreation. To those duties you have not yet been called, and when you are you will be less eager for celebrity.

ROBERT SOUTHEY

to Charlotte Brontë

229

The hardest thing for a man to do is to cope with feelings—his, yours, or anyone else's—so heaven forbid that you might confront him with the bad news that he's hurt you.

SONYA FRIEDMAN

I'd be willing to bet that if one day a woman walked barefoot to the moon and back and a man cleaned out his desk, when the two of them sat down to dinner that night, he would groan, "Boy, was that desk a mess."

MARGO KAUFMAN

Women, when they have made a sheep of a man, always tell him that he is a lion with a will of iron.

HONORÉ DE BALZAC

The fact of the matter is that the prime responsibility of a woman probably is to be on earth long enough to find the best mate possible for herself, and conceive children who will improve the species.

NORMAN MAILER

♂

The egotism of men surprises and shocks me even now. Is there a woman of my acquaintance who could sit in my armchair from 3 to 6:30 without the semblance of a suspicion that I may be busy, or tired, or bored; and so sitting could talk, grumbling and grudging of her difficulties, worries; then eat chocolates, then read a book, and go at last, apparently self-complacent and wrapped in a kind of blubber of misty self-satisfaction?

VIRGINIA WOOLF

♀

Seeing the great skill and accuracy with which these guys fly is something. There are a few ladies, but if God meant for ladies to fly he would have made the sky pink.

NICK SAUM

U.S. hot-air balloonist

♂

The male ego with few exceptions is elephantine to start with.

BETTE DAVIS

♀

Men read the woman's funny, ironic, and sometimes even sarcastic text as straight ("Oh, you're so strong. Can you really crush that beer can?") and are delighted to meet a woman who can finally "appreciate" them.

REGINA BARRECA

♂

. . . beware of men who cry. It's true that men who cry are sensitive to and in touch with feelings, but the only feelings they tend to be sensitive to and in touch with are their own.

NORA EPHRON

Women are much more like each other than men: they have, in truth, but two passions, vanity and love; these are their universal characteristics.

EARL OF CHESTERFIELD

He was like the cock who thought the sun had risen to hear him crow.

GEORGE ELIOT

Miss, n. A title with which we brand unmarried women to indicate that they are in the market. Miss, Missis (Mrs) and Mister (Mr) are the three most distinctly disagreeable words in the language, in sound and sense. Two are corruptions of Mistress, the other of Master . . . If we must have them, let us be consistent and give one to the unmarried man. I venture to suggest Mush, abbreviated to Mh.

AMBROSE BIERCE

When novelist Margaret Atwood asked women what they feared most from men, they replied, "We're afraid they'll kill us." When she asked men the same question about women, they replied, "We're afraid they'll laugh at us."

REPORTED BY NAOMI WOLF

Do you not know I am a woman? When I think, I must speak.

WILLIAM SHAKESPEARE

Although the father ranks above the mother, the mother has more to do with the offspring than the father has. Or we may say that woman was made chiefly in order to be man's helpmate in relation to the offspring, whereas the man was not made for this purpose. Wherefore the mother has a closer relation to the nature of marriage than the father has.

AQUINAS

Congress is a middle-aged, middle-class, white male power structure ... No wonder it's been so totally unresponsive to the needs of this country.

BELLA ABZUG

I will not say that women have no character; rather, they have a new one every day.

HEINRICH HEINE

If you talk about yourself, he'll think you're boring. If you talk about others, he'll think you're a gossip. If you talk about him, he'll think you're a brilliant conversationalist.

LINDA SUNSHINE

♂

Woman begins by
resisting a man's advances
and ends by blocking
his retreat.

OSCAR WILDE

♀

Hysteria is a natural phenomenon, the common denominator of the female nature. It's the big female weapon, and the test of a man is his ability to cope with it.

TENNESSEE WILLIAMS

There is so little difference between husbands you might as well keep the first.

ADELA ROGERS ST. JOHN

I think, Larissa," she said, "that all your strength comes precisely from your insecurity. It happens to a lot of women these days. It's not so much that we're striving to be strong ourselves, but the weakness of the men forces us to be. It's frightening how unmanly they have become. A husband in the home is just another child, only greedier."

YULIYA VOZNESENSKAYA

The Women's Decameron

I belong to Bridegrooms Anonymous. Whenever I feel like getting married, they send over a lady in a housecoat and hair curlers to burn my toast for me.

DICK MARTIN

A woman without a man is
like a fish without
a bicycle.

GLORIA STEINEM

Women are only children of a larger growth;
they have an entertaining tattle, and
sometimes wit, but for solid, reasoning good
sense, I never in my life knew one that had it.

LORD CHESTERFIELD

The fastest way to a man's heart is through his chest.

ROSEANNE ARNOLD

A woman is to be from her house three times: When she is christened, married, and buried.

ENGLISH PROVERB

The trouble with some women is that they get all excited about nothing—and then marry him.

CHER

Part Four: On Women

Tell a female she's thin and she's yours for life.

ANNE BERNAYS

Who does not tremble
when he considers how
to deal with a wife?

HENRY VIII

A woman always has her revenge ready.

MOLIÈRE

Tartuffe, II, ii

Women are strange and incomprehensible—invented by Providence to keep the wit of men well sharpened by constant employment.

ARNOLD BENNETT

A fickle thing and
changeful is woman
always.

VIRGIL

I'd much rather be a woman than a man. Women can cry, they can wear cute clothes, and they're first to be rescued off sinking ships.

GILDA RADNER

Every man who is high up likes to feel that he has done it himself; and the wife smiles, and lets it go at that.

J. M. BARRIE

♀

There are three things a woman can make out
of almost anything—a salad, a hat,
and a quarrel.

JOHN BARRYMORE

♂

Remember, Ginger Rogers did everything Fred Astaire did, but she did it backwards and in high heels.

FAITH WHITTLESEY

A liberated woman is one who has sex before marriage and a job after.

GLORIA STEINEM

Don't give a woman advice: one should never give a woman anything she can't wear in the evening.

OSCAR WILDE

Women run to extremes;
they are either better or
worse than men.

JEAN DE LA BRUYÈRE

When women go wrong, men go right after them.

MAE WEST

Between a woman's "yes"
and "no" I would not
venture to stick a pin.

MIGUEL DE CERVANTES

SAAVEDRA

Show me a woman who doesn't feel guilty and I'll show you a man.

ERICA JONG

A member of the British Parliament welcomed Lady Astor as she took her seat there on her first day as the first woman ever to be elected. "Welcome to the most exclusive men's club in Europe!" he said. "It won't be exclusive long," Lady Astor smiled. "When I came in, I left the door wide open!"

NANCY WITCHER LANGHORNE ASTOR

Fighting is essentially a masculine idea; a woman's weapon is her tongue.

HERMIONE GINGOLD

Women are hard enough
to handle now, without
giving them a gun.

SENATOR BARRY GOLDWATER

(on women in the military)

Some of us are becoming
the men we wanted
to marry.

GLORIA STEINEM

In all languages the words, Wife, Mother, are spoken with reverence, and associated with the highest, holiest functions of woman's earthly life. To man belongs the kingdom of the head: to woman the empire of the heart!

JAMES MCGRIGOR ALLAN

♂

The art of being a woman can never consist of being a bad imitation of a man.

OLGA KNOPF

Women are a lot like umpires. They make quick decisions, never reverse them, and they don't think you're safe when you're out.

PETE ROSE

♂

Whatever women do they must do twice as well as men to be thought half as good. Luckily, this is not difficult.

CHARLOTTE WHITTON

♀

It hurts me to confess it, but I'd have given ten conversations with Einstein for a first meeting with a pretty chorus girl.

ALBERT CAMUS

I always say it was great for God to send his only son, but I'm waiting for him to send his only daughter. Then things will really be great.

CANDACE PERT

Girls had it better from the beginning. Boys can run around fighting wars for made-up reasons with toy guns going kksshh-kksshh and arguing about who was dead, while girls play in the house with their dolls, creating complex family groups and solving problems through negotiation and role-playing. Which gender is better equipped, on the whole, to live an adult life, would you guess?

GARRISON KEILLOR

Did you ever hear of a great and good man who had not a good mother?

JOHN ADAMS

It has been women who have breathed gentleness and care into the harsh progress of mankind.

ELIZABETH II

There is no female mind. The brain is not an organ of sex. As well speak of a female liver.

CHARLOTTE PERKINS GILMAN

Even if you understood women—you'd never believe it.

FRANK DANE

♂

If I were asked to what the singular prosperity of the American people is to be mainly attributed, I should reply: to the superiority of their women.

ALEXIS DE TOCQUEVILLE

♀

The fundamental reason that women do not achieve so greatly as men do is that women have no wives.

PROFESSOR MARJORIE NICHOLSON

The phrase "working mother" is redundant.

JANE SELLMAN

Oh my son's my son till he gets him a wife,
But my daughter's my daughter all her life.

DINAH MARIA
MULOCK CRAIK

♂

She contradicts me even when I don't say anything!

BILL HOEST

There are only three things to be done with a woman. You can love her, you can suffer for her, or you can turn her into literature.

LAWRENCE DURRELL

The overemphasis on protecting girls from strain or injury and underemphasis on developing skills and experiencing teamwork fits neatly into the pattern of the second sex . . . Girls are the spectators and the cheerleaders . . . Perfect preparation for the adult role of woman—to stand decoratively on the sidelines of history and cheer on the men who make the decisions.

KATHRYN CLARENBACH

If only we could all accept that there is no difference between us where human values are concerned. Whatever sex.

LIV ULLMANN

The recognition by men that women are co-custodians of this planet, although absurdly belated, is one of the most hopeful developments in recent history.

CARL SAGAN

A woman is always buying something.

OVID

♂

♂

The old chestnut about women being more emotional than men has been forever destroyed by the evidence of the two world wars. Women under blockade, bombardment, concentration-camp conditions survive them vastly more successfully than men. The psychiatric casualties of populations under such conditions are *mostly* masculine.

ASHLEY MONTAGU

♀

**The hand that rocks the cradle
rules the world.**

PROVERB

How wrong it is for woman to expect the man to build the world she wants, rather than set out to create it herself.

ANAÏS NIN

Women have been in everything else—why not in politics? There's no reason why a woman shouldn't be in the White House as President, if she wants to be. But she'll be sorry when she gets there.

HARRY TRUMAN

♂

The way to fight a woman
is with your hat. Grab it
and run.

JOHN BARRYMORE

♀

Ideally, couples need three lives;
one for him, one for her, and one for each other.

JACQUELINE BISSET

. . . girls are so queer you never know what
they mean. They say No when they mean Yes,
and drive a man out of his wits
for the fun of it . . .

LOUISA MAY ALCOTT

Women are the real
architects of society.

HARRIET BEECHER STOWE

My true friends have always given me that supreme proof of devotion, a spontaneous aversion for the man I loved.

COLETTE

I do not believe that women are better than men. We have not wrecked railroads, nor corrupted legislatures, nor done many unholy things that men have done; but then we must remember that we have not had the chance.

JANE ADDAMS

The sort of woman who, if accidentally locked alone in the National Gallery, would start rearranging the pictures.

ANONYMOUS

The great truth is that
women actually like men,
and men can never
believe it.

ISABEL PATTERSON

Women upset everything. When you let them into your life, you find that the woman is driving at one thing and you're driving at another.

GEORGE BERNARD SHAW

Woman is the sun, an extraordinary creature, one that makes the imagination gallop. Woman is also the element of conflict. With whom do you argue? With a woman, of course. Not with a friend, because he accepted all your defects the moment he found you. Besides, woman is mother—have we forgotten?

MARCELLO MASTROIANNI

♂

If a man understands one woman he should let it go at that.

ROBERT CHAMBERS

"BOB" EDWARDS

♀

I know the influence of womanhood will guard the home, which is the citadel of the nation . . . I welcome it as a great instrument of mercy and a mighty agency of peace. I want every woman to vote.

CALVIN COOLIDGE

A girl can wait for the right man to come along but in the meantime that still doesn't mean she can't have a wonderful time with all the wrong ones.

C H E R

Being a woman is a terribly difficult trade, since it consists principally of dealing with men.

JOSEPH CONRAD

This is a time in history when women's voices must be heard, or forever be silenced. It's not because we think better than men, but we think differently. It's not women against men, but women and men. It's not that the world would have been better if women had run it, but that the world will be better when we as women, who bring our own perspective, share in running it.

BETTY BUMPERS

I think women are just as moved by appearance (as men are), but they are willing to accept a situation where the man is less attractive because of the who-earns-the-bread situation.

MADONNA

♂

**If the hours are long enough
and the pay is short enough,
someone will say it's
women's work.**

ANONYMOUS

♀

Women are not men's equals in anything
except responsibility. We are not their inferiors
either, or even their superiors. We are quite
simply a different race.

PHYLLIS MCGINLEY

Women who seek to be
equal with men
lack ambition.

TIMOTHY LEARY

♀

Of course men play roles, but women play roles too, blanker ones. They have, in the play of life, fewer good lines.

IRIS MURDOCH

♂

I wonder if what makes men walk lordlike and speak so masterfully is having the love of women.

ALMA ROUTSONG

Men fear women's strength.

ANAÏS NIN

Composing a piece of music is very feminine. It is sensitive, emotional, contemplative. By comparison, doing housework is positively masculine.

BARBARA KOLB

324

$♀$

Any woman who has a career and a family automatically develops something in the way of two personalities, like two sides of a dollar bill each different in design . . . Her problem is to keep one from draining the life from the other.

IVY BAKER PRIEST

$♂$

I think that implicit in the women's movement is the idea that women will share in the economic burden, and men will share more equally in the home and the family.

BETTY FRIEDAN

When men reach their sixties and retire, they go to pieces. Women go right on cooking.

GAIL SHEEHY

One of the things about equality is not just that you be treated equally to a man, but that you treat yourself equally to the way you treat a man.

MARLO THOMAS

Women have a passion for mathematics.
They divide their age in half, double the price
of their clothes, and always add at least five
years to the age of their best friend.

MARCEL ACHARD

What difference does it make whether women rule, or the rulers are ruled by women? The result is the same.

ARISTOTLE

One should never trust a woman who tells one her real age. A woman who would tell one that, would tell one anything.

OSCAR WILDE

♂

Who says women have to give up femininity to get equal legal rights? Anyway I don't want to go through a doorway ahead of a man—it's more fun to squeeze through together.

PERLE MESTA

♀

There will never be a new
world order until women
are a part of it.

ALICE PAUL

♂

**I know God is not a woman—
no woman would have created
men with so many
imperfections.**

JILL M. CONSIDEINE

♀

Tremendous amounts of talent are being lost to our society just because that talent wears a skirt.

SHIRLEY CHISHOLM

♂

By law, public sentiment, and religion from the time of Moses down to the present day, woman has never been thought of other than a piece of property, to be disposed of at the will and pleasure of man.

SUSAN B. ANTHONY

♀

**My advice to the women's clubs
of America is to raise more hell
and fewer children.**

AMES MCNEILL WHISTLER

I don't know any woman who doesn't feel guilty about something. That's the guilt gene, right?

HILLARY RODHAM
CLINTON

I hate women because they always know where things are.

JAMES "GROVER" THURBER

♂

The years that a woman subtracts from her age are not lost. They are added to the ages of other women.

DIANE DE POITIERS

♀

An attorney addressing the Supreme Court: "I would like to remind you gentlemen of a legal point." Justice O'Connor: "Would you like to remind me, too?"

SANDRA DAY O'CONNOR

Real equality is going to come not when a female Einstein is recognized as quickly as a male Einstein but when a female schlemiel is promoted as quickly as a male schlemiel.

BELLA ABZUG

A woman has got to love a bad man once or twice in her life, to be thankful for a good one.

MARJORIE KINNAN RAWLINGS

♂

No woman is all
sweetness; even the rose
has thorns.

MME. RECAMIER

The major concrete achievement of the women's movement in the 1970s was the Dutch treat.

NORA EPHRON

I earn and pay my own way as a great many women do today. Why should unmarried women be discriminated against—unmarried men are not.

DINAH SHORE

Don't let a man put anything over on you except an umbrella.

MAE WEST

♂

When a woman tells you her age it's all right to look surprised, but don't scowl.

—WILSON MIZNER

♀

The people I'm furious with are the women's liberationists. They keep getting up on soapboxes and proclaiming that women are brighter than men. It's true but it should be kept quiet or it ruins the whole racket.

ANITA LOOS

I never realized until lately that
women were supposed to be
the inferior sex.

KATHARINE HEPBURN

I'm not denyin' the
women are foolish: God
Almighty made 'em to
match the men.

GEORGE ELIOT

We are the grief of man, in that we take all the grief from man: we languish when they laugh, we lie sighing when they sit singing, and sit sobbing when they lie slugging and sleeping.

JANE ANGER

Woman, having received from her Creator
the same intellectual contribution as man, has
the same right as man to intellectual culture
and development.

MATTHEW VASSAR

353

Generally women are better than men—they have more character. I prefer men for some things, obviously, but women have a greater sense of honor and are more willing to take a chance with their lives. They are more open and decent in their relationship with a man. Men run all the time. I don't know how they live with themselves, they are so preoccupied with being studs.

LAUREN BACALL

If you educate a man you educate a person, but if you educate a woman you educate a family.

RUBY MANIKAN

A good woman inspires a man; a brilliant woman interests him; a beautiful woman fascinates him; and a sympathetic woman gets him.

HELEN ROWLAND

♀

Times change. Nowadays it's a woman who's faster on the draw, and she can prove it at any bank window.

ROY ROGERS

♂

Whether women are better than men I cannot say—but I can say they are certainly no worse.

GOLDA MEIR

♀

Never tell a woman she doesn't look good in some article of clothing she has just purchased.

LEWIS GRIZZARD

♂

I could have succeeded much easier in my career had I been a man.

HENRIETTA GREEN

Never go to bed mad.
Stay up and fight.

PHYLLIS DILLER

Men look *at* themselves in mirrors. Women look *for* themselves.

ELISSA MELAMED

An archeologist is the best husband a woman can have; the older she gets, the more interested he is in her.

AGATHA CHRISTIE

We are the loving sex; people count on us for comfort, nurturing, warmth. We hold the world together with the constant availability of our love when men would tear it apart with their needs for power.

NANCY FRIDAY

The reason good women like me and flock to my pictures is that there is a little bit of vampire instinct in every woman.

THEDA BARA

In revenge and in love
woman is more barbarous
than man.

FRIEDRICH NIETZSCHE

She plucked from my lapel the invisible
strand of lint (the universal act of woman
to proclaim ownership).

O . HENRY

As any psychologist will tell you,
the worst thing you can possibly do to
a woman is to deprive her of a grievance.

BEVERLY NICHOLS

Women want men, careers, money, children, friends, luxury, comfort, independence, freedom, respect, love, and a three-dollar panty hose that won't run.

PHYLLIS DILLER

♂

My wife doesn't care what I do
when I'm away, as long as I
don't have a good time.

LEE TREVINO

I do not believe in using
women in combat, because
females are too fierce.

MARGARET MEAD

Basically my wife was immature. I'd be at home in the bath and she'd come in and sink my boats.

WOODY ALLEN

♀

**A woman's guess is
much more accurate than
a man's certainty.**

RUDYARD KIPLING

♂

This book was typeset in
Kabel Book, Demi, and Ultra.

Book design and typesetting by
Judith Stagnitto Abbate

Cover illustration by Debra Solomon

Cover design by Sara Stemen